The Colourful Life!
Same but different

Naomi Kissiedu-Green

All rights reserved. No part of this book may be reproduced or transmitted in any form or by any means, electronic or mechanical, including photocopying, recording, or by an information storage and retrieval system - except by a reviewer who may quote brief passages in a review to be printed in a magazine or newspaper - without permission in writing from the publisher.

copyright © 2013 Naomi Kissiedu Green

All rights reserved.

ISBN-13: 978-0994465603

DEDICATION

I dedicate this book firstly to myself! I put so much hard work and dedication into this for you to read. I believed in myself and my commitment. I believe you must have faith in yourself and do the things you love.

There are friends and family members who also encouraged me to take the plunge - you know who you are – and to them I offer my heartfelt gratitude.

And to all of you who can relate to this book: **you are unique.**

NOTES FOR TEACHER OR PARENT

I write these books for children entering day care or pre-school who are becoming aware of the world outside of their families for the first time. They might notice things about people – like someone's skin being different in hue from theirs or a baby growing inside a mother's "tummy". Since children are curious, they may ask, "What's in your tummy?" or "Why is my skin different from yours?"

I hope both parents and children are helped by the answers provided within my books.

When reading the stories, you may wish to ask your children about the identity depicted. Find out what your children's thoughts are about the different identities.

Exploring together the stories scenarios will help children develop a better understanding of life's complexities and help them feel more settled and secure in themselves and their situation.

Same, but different

This is a story about a boy called Kobi and his family. Kobi is mixed race and there are not many families like Kobi's where Kobi lives. Kobi's teacher, with the help of Kobi's parents, shows Kobi and his class that people can appear different, but they also very often have a lot in common. Together Kobi and his classmates learn to accept that everyone is different… but in some respects, they are also the same.

ACKNOWLEDGMENTS

I would like to express my gratitude to the many people who helped to carry me through this book. To all those who read, wrote, offered comments, and assisted in the editing, proofreading and illustrations, I offer my heartfelt gratitude.

And to my children, my darlings, I love you. You are my ultimate creations.

I am all things sweet, all things nice.

I am a bit of chocolate. I am a bit of vanilla.

I am a caramel delight.

I am a child of mixed heritage. My mother is black and my father is white. My skin is the perfect mix of both; it has a smooth brown tone that represents the heritage of each of my parents. I have brown, curly, afro hair and big brown eyes. I am neither black nor white. I am mixed race and proud to be.

I am constantly asked, "What are you?"

What am I? Who am I? I will tell you. My name is Kobi, and I am five years old. I live in Australia with my family. In Australia, there are not many children that look like me and there are few families like mine. When I go to kindergarten, kids stop and stare! Sometimes, they point and whisper as my family and I walk by.

Today, both my parents brought me to school. I kissed them goodbye and headed towards the playground to play with some of my classmates.

Jacob, one of the kids in my class, asked me, "Who brought you to school today, Kobi? Are those people your parents?"

I said "Yes, that's my Mummy and Daddy." Jacob was shocked. He and the other kids in the playground did not believe me.

"But the lady is black and the man is white? How can that be? You don't have the same colour as either of them. Those people are NOT your parents!" Jacob shouted.

Jacob's remarks made me sad, so I ran back to my parents. When Mummy saw my sad face she walked towards me with her arms opened wide. I gave her a big hug and buried my face in her chest. She pulled me back, looked at me and said, "Stop crying and tell me what happened." I told her what Jacob had said. She looked at me sympathetically.

"Kobi, don't cry. You are beautiful. We love you. You are a perfect mix of Daddy and me. You are unique. Sometimes when people don't understand something that is different from them, they say mean things. It will make you angry and even sad. But instead of crying, you must hold up your head. Tell your friends how proud you are to be part of a beautiful, blended family. Tell them that you are incredibly special."

After my talk with Mummy, I felt a lot better. I walked with her over to my teacher Mrs. Laryea. Mrs Laryea is tall, slim and has a dark complexion. She wears big round glasses and long plaits in her hair that stretch all the way down her back.

Mrs. Laryea and Mummy began speaking so I headed to class. As I walked away, Mummy told me that she would be back very soon.

The lesson begins

Class began soon after and Mrs. Laryea invited me to stand in front of the class. The other children were seated around their tables talking, laughing and playing with each other. Moments later, the classroom was quiet.

"Let me introduce you to some of your new friends," Mrs. Laryea said.

"Do you see the boy at the back of the room with blond curly hair? His name is Charlie. The boy next to him, Oliver, he has blue eyes. The girl sitting at the front of the class, her name is Emma. You can see that she has brown, curly, afro hair just like you Kobi.

Today I am going to teach you about things that are the same, but different. Here are a few things that are different about you and your friends. For example, Emma is a girl… and you are?" she turned to ask me.

"I'm a boy!" I replied, quite sure that I had that answer right.

"Oliver sometimes wears glasses. Do you?" Mrs. Laryea asked me.

I shook my head fiercely.

"Charlie, what's your favorite colour?"

"Blue," replied Charlie, grinning.

"What's your favorite colour, Kobi?" my teacher asked.

I thought for a moment then I replied, "I like blue too, but I think green is my favorite colour, just like my surname."

"So, those are just a few things about us that aren't the same. As you can see we are different. Let's see if we can find some things about us that are the same," said Mrs. Laryea.

"Emma is wearing the same boots as whom?"

We all looked at Emma's brown leather boots with thick brown laces. I smiled, and before I could say anything, someone shouted. "Emma is wearing the same boots as Kobi!"

Emma lifted her boot to mine, and we laughed. We had the same boots indeed.

Next, Oliver came over to me and said. "Kobi and I are the same height. We stood back-to-back as Mrs. Laryea measured us. We were indeed the same height.

"What else do you like, Kobi?" asked my teacher.

"I like cars," I said.

"Me too!" said Charlie. "I love cars. I have about 15 different cars. You should bring your cars to my house, and we can play with them," he said.

I smiled. "I will, but I have to ask my Mum and Dad."

Mrs. Laryea then asked us to think about our families and think of things that were the same and that were different.

My mother has afro curly hair and big brown eyes just like me. Her skin is brown and her hair color is black. My father has straight brown hair. He also has big eyes but his eyes are blue, and he has pale milky skin.

Surprise visitors

Suddenly the classroom door opens. In walk my Mummy and Daddy. I can't help but smile. But I am also a bit confused; it definitely isn't time for recess. My parents then walk to the front of the class.

"Hello everyone, I am Kobi's Mum. This is his Dad."

My dad waves and some of the kids wave back.

"Come over to me and hold out your hands," my Mum instructs the children.

The children excitedly walk towards my mother. Some are a bit nervous, not knowing what to expect. We all hold out our hands just like Mummy told us to do. "Put your hands next to mine and Kobi's dad's".

Everyone does as Mummy asks. "Now, pay attention to the colour of your skin. Look at everyone else's and tell me what you see."

Everyone looks at their hands, then at the other hands held out in front of them. "Mummy, your skin is brown, just like Emma's and mine," I say.

"That's right Kobi, but are our hands the same shade?" Mummy says.

"No!" shouts Oliver from the front row. "Kobi's skin is lighter than his mother and Emma is darker than Kobi."

Then my mummy turns to Charlie, the boy with the curly blonde hair and asks, "What about the colour of your skin? You are lighter than Oliver. Oliver is darker than you. But are you lighter than Kobi's dad, Charlie, or darker?" Mummy asks.

We all spend a bit of time with my Mummy and Daddy looking at the different shades of our skin. "As you can see, we don't all have exactly the same complexion. We all have things that are the same and things that are different. We are all unique and special," Daddy says to everyone.

Same but Different

I am absolutely thrilled that my parents came to school. I am even more proud of who I am. Now all my classmates understand that I am of mixed race and even though my parents and I are different colours, we are still a loving, happy family.

People are made up of all different shades of colour. Families sometimes don't always look alike, but they are still a family. We are all so different, but we are the same, too. We are all beautiful because we are all unique.

Draw your unique family here.

Did I tell you that my mummy is pregnant? That means she is having a baby. I am very excited. I will tell my baby that they are beautiful and unique too. Whether the baby is a boy or a girl, or whether the same or different, I know my mummy and daddy will love us both no matter what!

ABOUT THE AUTHOR

I am a wife and mother who relishes bringing my ideas and passion to life.

In my capacity as mother and qualified childcare worker I have been disheartened to discover the paucity of resources that cater to multicultural families in Australia. It can be a struggle to find books to read to your children that depict multicultural families – or even families of other cultures. I honestly wish there were more representations of cultures and mixed race people in the media.

So I wrote this book for multiracial families like mine, and other families who want to embrace diversity and acceptance. It's important for children to see themselves as they develop a sense of community and belonging. It is our responsibility – as parents and as a nation – to make children feel included not just in their home, but in the classroom and in life.

Racial and ethnic group differences have a significant impact on children's social development. Although the impact varies according to age and ethnicity, it is important for children to take pride in their heritage.

I hope to shine a spotlight on the issue of mixed race with my Kobi books, and offer something to multiracial families with which they can identify.

Same but Different

www.ingramcontent.com/pod-product-compliance
Lightning Source LLC
Chambersburg PA
CBHW061931290426
44113CB00024B/2877